MEPHISTOPHELES

First published in 2023 by Blue Diode Press
30 Lochend Road
Leith
Edinburgh EH6 8BS
www.bluediode.co.uk

ISBN: 978-1-915108-16-6

Typesetting: Rob A. Mackenzie
text in Dante MT Pro

Cover art: Rebecca Scott
Cover design: CD Boyland, Rob A. Mackenzie

Diode logo design: Sam and Ian Alexander

Printed and bound by Imprint Digital, Exeter, UK.
https://digital.imprint.co.uk

MEPHISTOPHELES

CD Boyland

BLUE DIODE PRESS
Edinburgh

Hell is empty and all the devils are here.

The Tempest

That melancholy, tortured, and surprisingly truthful fiend,
Mephistopheles.

John D. Jump

Contents

The War in Heaven (after Milton)

[T]he massacre in heaven || which some people have mistaken || for a battle || which some people have mistaken || for a war || which presumes that there were || two sides fighting || featured chariots & fiery steeds || & third person fixed cinematic cameras || marginalising dissent through || the use of distracting theatrics || & a pounding techno soundtrack || reinforcing the dominant value system || with the exception of the || 'Mount of God' side-mission || which included bonus questions about || thrones & dominions || & themes from earlier conflicts || characterised by forces of reaction || armed in adamant & gold || dominated by horrible discord || & madding wheels || ignoring whether it was ever || a fair go or an even fight || or any such nonsense || a departure from the || usual 2-D scrolling syntax || & helmets thronged & shields various || 'beat-em up' combat || & puzzle game elements || from the footage broadcast || on televisions around the world || the massacre was packed full || of incident & trauma || yet for a dance it seemed || somewhat extravagant & wild || there was little evidence of resistance || weapons deployed varied in gameplay || & levels of deliberate carnage || magic was also used || to provide justification || for the slaughter || & to censor & suppress || any sympathy for the massacred || chariots & charioteers overturned || could be recharged || by combinations of coloured orbs || & charred corpses leaning || from bomb-blasted screens || our rebellion did not finish || in an optional fight || with an end-level guardian || love was our final resistance || before the fall.

The Beach

[T]wo hundred or so years ago
or maybe yesterday
Johann Goethe stumbles out of the sea
rolls onto his back
a Gutenberg bible lodged between his sixth & seventh vertebrae
jaws distended, screams –

his voice achieves acoustic velocity
a signal seeking noise
born upon waves of angelic interference
reinforcement patterns of Bach & Godel
up into the firmament, further still

somewhere past the rings of Saturn
intercepts a wandering asteroid
the nascent idea of Babbage's difference engine
algorithms for keyword search
encoded in its ferrous core
the DNA of microchips hidden beneath its skirts
they whisper love-songs to each other in base 16
to the tune of 'La Vie En Rose'

Goethe's body ossifies, turns fossil
gives up its legion of foreign ghosts
radiates presumptions of industry, the masses at their toil
the steady tick of geiger time, raising the temperature
an infinite half-life, pregnant with coal & deep-sea oil
the slow beat of his concrete heart
frightens the birds.

The Agency

[V]oice in your ear, that
wire taped to the small of
your back, runs down
the margin of this page

pulls your head upright
as if (*as if?*) your spine is a
hinge & not some
tired metaphor for courage

black box clipped
to your waistband, red light
unblinking

You know what you're
supposed to be doing, how
you're supposed to be
behaving but are the rules

you're following R*eal?*
Imaginary? Symbolic?
& how much of a kicking
will you get from the Chief, if
you guess wrong, pal?

See that way you talk, we
taught you that, we put the
words in order, wrote
them down, made you repeat

them back to us, that's
your voice on the tape
howling like a monkey
but you don't know why
you said those things

There's a name for
people like you, think they
can play outside the
law, take on the system, beat

Big Other at his own
game but I'm here to tell
you, pal – the elevators
go sideways, up & down

& whatever belief
system you're working to, it's
all up *here*, the fight
was rigged before you even

got on the board, pal
you're a horse's head that wants
to be a castle but that's
not a choice you get to make.

Prologue in Heaven

[I]n the name of the Father
unbothered by their
blasphemous levity, stepping
down from the heavenly sphere
they meet up for a drink

Jesu raises a glass
mindful of wounds in palms
not to bleed on His white robe
St Michael's spear propped carelessly
beside the open door

universal English faces
more human than divine, by order
exchanging pre-Babylonian banter
beneath their table, the Devil writhes
& begs for scraps, gets nothing

Other punters in the bar
mindful of their mortality
keep a nervous distance
wary of light unapproachable
how men, being life-size only
are all too easily trodden beneath
their saviour's feet.

The Shape

[**D**]ig || beneath the skin || apply your tools || some ancient || the knapped flint cutting edge || some modern || or yet to be designed || unearth the architecture || of language || its striated layers || your fixation with dead empires || write down what you see || proceed further || to the atomic level || admire the constellation || of its connections || the voyage of argon || along the capillaries of time || visit the far-flung outposts || of this diaspora || plot them on a map || consider the outline || you have drawn || its shape || what it reminds you of || is it a man?

The Body

[S]tuff
the entirety of man
& womankind into the
singular body of *this* man
& see what happens –

– watch his belly distend
in folds down to his ankles
to accommodate our
        hunger –

– behind the buttons of
his waistcoat, so many
varied interests & perspectives
find common ground or
        go to war –

– beneath a neatly brushed
& levelled hat, his psoriatic
scalp breaks out into a map of
all the places he has never
        lived –

– between his shoulder-blades
a chimney rises, from whence
the ashes of unnumbered hearths
are vented – make him sing some
of the songs once sung before
those hearths, see how well he
knows the words –

– find room, if you can
on his pale skin, amongst
the stubborn tufts of greying

hair, to write the names of
all the dead & all their stories –
one skin sloughs off, either
in embarrassment or shame –

– keep writing, cover the
fresh pink epidermis with
words & numbers & then
when that moults off, begin
the next –

– press the discarded hides
between covers, start a
library.

The Bells

[B]right notes || force from your lips || the lifted glass || a good job is near impossible || for someone like you to find || making money anyway you can || beneath it all || the love of music || arms outstretched || songs of heaven || a change in the chemical weather || hitting like a paycheque cashed || arriving full of kindness || to find you || thoughts dissolving || fractal catechisms recited || in other peoples' voices || daisy chains of glow stick smiles || choirs of angels drifting gently || clouds of *Alleluias* || come to seek you in the dark || calling you to life again || no regrets || no scars || fingers pointing || & everybody's wings are beating || the kiss of heaven's love upon you || Memnosyne loves music best || of all her children || & all the ways she's just not into you || don't matter || because *'man, I fucking love this tune!'* || meeting Selene || in the back-seat of a late-night taxi || & everyone's connected || lost in a maze || of breakbeat sonics || microdots receding in their eyes || folding these feelings || smaller & smaller & smaller || 'til they're just a weight || of light inside you || admiring the view || from the window of || a departing Perseid || & you are || as deep as you breathe || roots tapped into immortal mud || & something is coming || weep || for you are the earth again || someone is coming || & there is magic || in the way she braids her hair.

The Red Pill

[I]s to dispute well logic's chiefest end?   [y/n]
is philosophy odious & obscure?   [y/n]

is our body's health the end of physic
have you (**F**) not achieved that end?   [y/n]
yet are still but (**F**), & a man?   [y/n]

does the study of law fit a mercenary drudge
who aims at nothing but external trash?   [y/n]
are law & physic both for petty wits?   [y/n]

is death the reward of sin?   [y/n]
is there no truth in us, if we say we have no sin?   [y/n]
is it therefore, that we must sin & so, consequently, die?   [y/n]

do you (**F**), grounded in astrology, enriched with tongues
well seen in minerals, have all the principles magic doth
require?   [y/n]

& if you (**F**) will be resolute, will spirits of every
element be always serviceable to you (**F**)?   [y/n]

will they guard you (**F**) like lions when you please?   [y/n]
will they drag huge argosies from Venice & America
the golden fleece that yearly stuffs old Philip's treasury?   [y/n]
will they dry the sea & fetch the treasure of all foreign
wrecks?   [y/n]

will the miracles that magic may perform make you (**F**)
vow to study nothing else?   [y/n]

will you (**F**) conjure though you die therefor?   [y/n]

If [y] then what shall you (**F**) want?

Mephistopheles

[H]ow should I arrive, my love   my love, should I arrive?
In four or three dimensions fold   my body to your room?
Leather mask kimono mirror   belief is to undress
Countenance bleed body shape   excite the man tonight
Meat-suit worn in servitude   draws favour on your love
Ignite conspire indignities lips   bruise your fist, my slave

Naked nothing personal be   obliged a master's slave
No agency may cancel fire   that spies when I arrive
Wake sanity offence besmirch   cheap physics in the room
Insult your hungry mouths to   suckle my impure address
Burnished silk kimono loins   stalk tigers in the night
Unwilling camera's exposé   will piss on you, my love

In ribbons' harnessed tribute be   a floorshow for my love
Night drips greedy perfume to   anoint you as my slave
Clock-waisted hours conjoin   kimono's silk when I arrive
Enchantment needless effigy   my tricks delight the room
Opening & fumbling hands   forbid harshly to undress
Coordinates for treason mark   a wedding feast tonight

Tapes kimono blasphemy in   witness ears tonight
Firelight is willing torment   bleed anything but love
Master sanity clause invokes   tears up another slave
Take tea with heresy & burn   all books when I arrive
Delicacies like oyster cunts   your bourgeois little room
Alchemical well-heeled hump   silver pours into my dress

A martyr's cause for burning   tribute paid for in redress
All souls disposed of urgently   support the cause tonight
Encampment on escarpment   melts rocks before my love
Gaze lowered kimono viciously   up-sleeve the brand of slave
Cruelty of devils uncocked   extort my sex when I arrive
Windows draw the night into   this mausoleum of a room

I'll undress you at your books
Sate thirst for burning effigies
Kimono chair silk stockings call
Whatever untapped blasphemy
Bitter fruit taste iron chains
So how should I arrive, my love

shred music in your room
ignite trespass in my dress
His name in vain tonight
conjures the marks of love
abhor your bondage slave
my love, should I arrive

In traitor's shape, should I arrive
In nanite spider womb silk dress
In effigy abandoned love to ask

on pages of your room
to wear your curse tonight
which of us is the slave?

The Interview

[C]an
you tell
me
about
a time
when you
consumed fuel –
refined petroleum
wood
the bones
of that Midlands
cathedral
– can you tell me
about your
exothermic marriage
the begetting
of your children – heat &
light
the ecstasy of
transformation from fossil to
combustion
can you tell me about a time
you hid   beneath
banked peats, a red-eyed
red-toothed creature
awaiting bellowed breath
the kiss   of oxygen
an instant of
Pentecostal transformation
hymned by tongues
of orange   flame – *dance,*
then, wherever you may be
I am   the Lord of the
dance, said he

– can you tell me   about
          the taste of forests
          the indigestibility of   stone
how it feels   to be born from coal
to rage for one   blind moment
          on the earth & scorch
          the ground beneath you?

The Fall

[**B**]eing eye of mind
dream of sorcery made real

being eye of sum of parts
sensations & ideals

given body & mind to
a message, some design that

trapped inside your body's story
decidedly dependent on context
dear heart

being distance from the sun
being what you hold ideal

being explosion of pent-up
　　　　energies

being what you bring to this
　　　　party, Faustus my love

being what you choose

　　or

give no purpose to your flight

& being empty vessel –

embrace of hidden arts
greater & greater & greater

escaping Wittenberg
born upon these wings

lift you heavenwards &
puts 'this' into words but

hubris, fate, lessons ignored,

being distance from your god
being what holds you aloft

being urge to escape history
occurring within history

being what has meaning

being the choice – to break
out of the pleasure-prison
detention-context
controlling leisure-system –

attach no meaning to what
lifts you to these heights

　　　　　　fall.

The Morning

[A]fterwards, I wrote my name in delicate filigree traces on the inside of his eyelids & showed him my tattoos. As we lay together, the ink wept from my skin, made new images on the sheets, mixing with his sweat & spent fluids. On my back, the gates of Hell beckoned warmly, an acknowledgement – I am a doorway, through me ye may enter. Down my legs, black roots writhed & stretched, for I am a flower of the deep, deep Earth & the sun which warms your skin will never find me. On my belly, I'd drawn his face – for I am a mirror, in me, ye may see yrself as ye truly are. He lay beside me, watched his various futures come to pass, inscribed across the soft contours of my body, all his sweet & terrible endings, alive with subcutaneous colours. 'What would I be without you?', he wondered out loud 'other than a man'.

The Box

[**U**]npack this box || which is a man || rummage through its contents || memories || emotional states || a big sack of something || sloshing about || labelled 'identity' || something wet & sticky || leaking out || smells a little off || 'Pride' – *blah, blah* || a complicated unfolding || assemblage of clockwork || called a 'belief system' || battered, dusty || not sure if it || still works || various ideas about || physical attractiveness || some of them fair || most not || empty the box || something's missing || turn it upside down || shake vigorously || nothing.

Farewell

[**D**]ry your eyes my sweet, it's too late now, farewell
to pride & riches & those stolen summer kisses
men who laugh on earth are fools that weep in Hell

can you hear the tolling of a crack'd & distant bell
it knows your name & all the wrongs you've done
dry your eyes my sweet, it's much too late, farewell

cast aside your property & all that useless wealth
barter everything you are for one last moment's light
men who laugh on earth are fools that weep in Hell

empty your soul of music & forgo its joyful swell
all those weary lullabies, you supposed were hymns
dry your eyes my sweet, it's too late now, farewell

strip away your selfishness, stand naked in your cell
leave your pride & vanity in tatters on the floor
men who laugh on earth are fools that weep in Hell

you were just an empty thing, a hollow wasted shell
did you once believe you were the hero of this tale?
dry your eyes my sweet, it's much too late, farewell
men who laugh on earth are fools that weep in Hell.

The Algorithm

5	[**B**]ind yourself
6	PRINT I offer you this wager
10	LET C = [lying flattery]
20	LET D = [settle upon a bed of ease]
30	INPUT A [all kinds of wonder]
40	INPUT B [pleasure that hurts most]
50	COMPUTE A + B
60	IF (A + B) = C THEN GOTO 30
70	IF (A + B) ≠ C THEN GOTO 80
80	IF (A + B) = D THEN GOTO 90
90	LET Faust end his days
100	END

A generalised process for
the creation of outputs from
inputs

– input parameters being arbitrary &
infinite in extent or limited in extent
but still changeable (like man) –

by manipulation of symbols
according to finite collections of rules

that a person may perform with
paper & pen (or write with blood upon
a parchment)

The Wager

[B]ide here   you are so beautiful
a nightingale   nested in your breast
tell the world   to stop, rest & be
thankful, feel   everything's in its
right place   unfold the possibilities
of joy, set free   the fiddle's sky bound
song, take time   for yourself – seems
such a moment   of happiness, a whisper
of bright light   that beckons you, *linger*
yet you are so fair   ought to be the prize
itself & not the   losing of it – don't you
     think?

The Engine

[T]hat turns & never rests
from one day to the next
from peak to peak of
never rests, that chains
make all power unleashed
the kindling & never rests
fire of great & ever-greater
augmenting & improving
around connects more
yielding deeper harmony
humankind & never rests
things & changes him from

that runs with ever greater speed
& never rests, that powers flight
ever more surpassing height &
such energies tomorrow as
today seem like a spark amongst
to be an engine driven by the
passion that never rests, that by
his innermost self & all the world
levels & interstices of the cosmos
& more profound alignment between
an engine which does all these
what he is, to what he is but

more so.

The Dolls

[T]he room   has a bunk with two sheets

The room   has a door with an observation window

The room   is empty, or

The room   is cluttered with mannequins of various kinds –
dolls, shop window dummies, puppets collapsed
in their tangled strings

The dolls   speak to him or so he believes

The dolls   are piled in heaps, some of them broken or

The dolls   are organised into groups or tableau – in one
corner, Pope Adrian climbs from Bruno's back
to St Peter's chair. In another, Alexander & his
paramour salute the German Emperor

The dolls   occasionally appear in other rooms in the
hospital, or so the janitorial staff believe.
None of them are ever found or brought to the
attention of the authorities.

One day   we find him pressed up against the far wall of
his cell – the dolls, he says, have filled the rest of
the space so completely there is no room for
him to move, barely room to breathe.

One day   he is rapt in conversation with a ragged cloth
doll that he calls 'Mephistopheles', so engrossed
that he does not notice or lift his head when we
enter the room

One day	he is offended by the presence of one of our students & curses him. The young man wakes up the next day with a full spread of horns clapped upon his head, or
One day	he is offended by the presence of one of our students, a young man by the name of 'Mephistopheles'. We change his medication
The years	pass, none of our treatments seem to have any effect, his condition deteriorates, or
The years	pass, he responds well to his treatment, or
The years	pass, funding for our treatment programme is cut, our patients are released back into society, to fend for themselves as best they can, or
The years	pass.

The Tavern

[**W**]herein Marlowe & Goethe
glower at each other from
either side of their table, plates
of bread & dishes of pickled
herring between them, half-empty
bottle of vodka close at hand
'Faustus be damned', cries one
(I need not say who), 'Faust be
saved by virtue of his industry &
mighty works', shouts the other –

  – '& that' observes
Tsvetaeva from a table
nearby, 'says more about
the pair of you than it does
about what matters to the
              rest of us'.

Jan Twardowski

[A]nother rogue, crown
& gold leaf, sailed
kettle with the holy
cabin boy, stood
fire for too long &
lick the goose-fat
his fingers, black
the nails, his laboratory
of glass tubes, beakers
hose, he'd mix the
heat the dose over a
out, whispering
a dead hare, glaring
tartan blanket he wore
play a mean blues
was in the mood
vodka poured from
shoemaker or sign
written on bull's hide
it was just questions

painted with honey
to the moon in a tea
virgin Mary as his
with his back to the
burnt his arse, liked to
from the dish, blistered
sickles of dirt beneath
was a baboon's fantasy
copper pipes & rubber
shot in a silver spoon
Bunsen burner & nod
ballads into the ear of
at me from over the
like a shroud, he'd
harmonica when he
fill your cup with
the ear of a whiskered
his name to a cryograph
but most of the time
questions questions.

Hey ayya-ayya hey. Hey ay-ah. Hey
Hey ayya-ayya hey. Hey ay-ah.

The Show

[**S**]hape – showman – shifter
  showgirl? show-woman?
  & the divide between that & *that,* my pretty –
  & who wears the stockings, disports
  themself in high-heeled boots, the better
  to show off their elegant calves –

come into my tent & see
  back straight, tits out
  a little mascara for the eyes, some
  oil for the beard, all primped & combed

beneath my red coat, its pattern
  cunningly picked out in black & gold
  beneath the sass & swish of my
  taffeta skirts –

a world of wonders awaits, come see
  come see – a universe of marvels
  on the back of a flea, intricacies
  of atomic clockwork, filigreed &
  plated just so, pathogenetic armies
  marshalled beneath glass, that can
  be borne upon a finger-tip – yet when
  unleashed could topple proud Perse-
  polis in but a single day – come see –

come wander, through this cabinet of miracles
  step between the pools of golden
  light cast by a myriad of bejewelled
  lanterns, stroll beneath the arc-lamps
  standing sentinel on towers above
  the wire fences, ask not what goes
  on in the shadows, what fuel is burned

to power the generators that vent
their noxious smoke into the firmament

   – come see the elephant, follow
its dancing skeleton, its top hat
jauntily askew, fall in with the
cadence of its ebony cane tap-
tapping on the boards, laugh at
        its jokes –

on with the show.

The Seven Sins

[I] am pride. My mother was a flag & my father stood before her to salute, wearing his pale skin like a medal of empire. I am all the statues raised to men long since forgotten & those who gather before them with their arms crossed like rifles are my children. I have built my house on the deeds of others & in it I have placed an altar to myself. Prick me & see me swell like an engorged cock, for I am the empty vessel that rings loudest when it is softest struck.

I am anger & my mouth is a closed fist & the words I spit at you are stones & bricks & both my hands are batons, the better to beat you with when you are down, the better to strike you with when your back's turned, when there's nothing you can do to fight back. I am the graffiti on your door & all the anonymous voices on the phone that threaten your children, & I am as strong as I can pretend to be so long as there are more of me than there are of you.

I am lust & I am unashamed & why should I be otherwise? It's not me imagining what's beneath this T-shirt or begging for candid selfies. Not me who always needs to click onto another image, another video, another page. I'm not the private members' area in your dreams, the iron door with its velvet key, the spiked collar you've strapped around your needs. I'm a good fuck & a good lay, a warm body in a cosy bed. I'm into what you're into, so long as you're honest with me.

I am avarice & I was born in the small print, the child of a service charge & an over-leveraged acquisition. I have never seen currency I didn't want to exchange for collateralised debt obligations, to offset against credit default swaps, to hedge against the price of a man's soul. I wrote the rent on my mother's womb off against tax & used the additional liquidity to starve a small country into conceding its mineral rights to my corporate interests. I have as many fingers as there are pies & all of my children own bakeries.

I am gluttony & that was me last night, pissing through your letterbox. I dredged the river bed to buy a brewery & when they called 'time', I lay down with my mouth beneath the tap & drank the barrel dry. I'm funny as fuck when I'm sober which is why all my friends are whisky bottles, even the empty ones. I've rolled home more times than there are stones in the road & that's how I came by this cork in my mouth & these stains on my trousers. I'm lost without a glass in my hand & here's how you find me, dry as a judge's wig & shamefully short of a drink.

I am envy & I've been watching, creeping up your windows like a fly, spying on your children & that lovely little wife. I'd have a bride like her if you didn't keep coming round like winter, stealing the good things & hiding them all away. I know what she's keeping in her knickers & I'll get at it one day. I'll be in through the keyhole of the next house too, counting all their pretty things. Doesn't matter what it is, it's always better when it's someone else's, like butter on toast, you have to lick it up where it's been dripping.

I am sloth & there's only one of me so it really doesn't matter & it won't make a difference. I didn't come to the meeting because I was sleeping under a pile of all the votes I've never cast or making a list of the books I could have written if I'd just unsewn my hands from these pockets & spent less time in the long line of people who said there's no point trying because nothing really changes & that's why I'm here, lying like a snowdrift up against everything & I'd get out of your way but it's just too much trouble.

The Witch's Kitchen

[W]orm my way in
stiffen, little worm
straighten that limp
between your legs
an unholy 'yes'
this sun & moon &
of philosophy &
dirty with it, roll
selves, on a scale
one is 'sub' & ten
like this apple, little
rich, dark earth, a
together, you &
truthfully, is she
of paradise, don't
something pretty
don't you want to
mouth, tell her what
on a scale of one to
everything, what
that sweet body, to
very own, open wide
swallow this pill &
Helen for you, so
session, undress her
her kneel, spill your

worm my way out
let's see if we can't
question that hangs
into an exclamation
 let's get past all of
stars, the mysteries
let's get down &
around in our naked
of one to ten, where
is 'dom', how do you
man, grown in the
bed where we can lie
I, tell the mirror
not quintessence
you want to buy her
from her wish-list
play Pinochle in her
to do & what to say
ten, where one is
would you give for
have her for your
now, my brave man,
I'll wear the shape of
you can enjoy a private
as you please, make
seed on her perfect tits.

Greta (after Mayakovsky)

[C]arousing in your apartment on Zhukovsky
street, dancing amongst the ziggurats of an
unfolding future & the tea-cups, your face
is a wiring-diagram for an electric engine of
potential. I have tried to draw you so many
times but you keep bursting from the frame
dashing off to the shops for melons & wild
cherries, bathing in the yellow light of trains
migrating like a swallow to Africa – yellow
will always & forever be your colour, the
insouciance of it, the way it dances across
tram-lines in the street & needs no passport
you have forgiven all the sins of this dying
age, you are its first & final admonishment.

Helen

[Y]ou tore your own shadow off the wall & stuffed it
in a tote bag so there would be nothing left behind you

– got used to living how & where you could, landing on
couches in freezing Bushwick railroads with bathroom
ceilings that wept admonitory tears

– part of an industry that fetishised the production of
newness but followed the narrative arc of classical
drama

– while topless towers of Ilium burned in night vision on TV
between commercials for Diet Tab & MAC cosmetics

– & everyone complained about the death of film

– you put on your wedding gown stained with the blood
of infants & walked out the door

– while tubby Menelaus gibbered between set-ups, about
antibiotics he was taking for recurrent bouts of gonorrhoea

– & assistants struck the set & packed the couture gowns
leaving no visible wounds, no arrowheads to be recovered
from the grave

– you offered up your book as if believing it comprised
all your achievements

– told you were more lovely than the monarch of the sky,
something about wanton Aresthusa's azure'd arms, wearing
dresses that cost $29,000 mostly constructed of ostrich feathers

– while managing on a budget of $80 per week doled out as weekly loans which they insisted on calling 'pocket money'

– & being kept endlessly occupied but bored

– you enjoyed constant contact with lovely women, smart women, talented women, hard-working women, inspiring women, women you wanted to grow up to be.

– while walking between castings & going to 5 or 10 different addresses every day

– & stumbling home at a quarter to five in the morning

– you stayed up late, talking about Lech Walesa & the problems of teaching post-WWII history

– living in Pepto-Bismol wombs in Paris that gave you pregnancy nightmares

– & being the kind of person who didn't recognise when a teenager was injecting Class A narcotics

– you kept your own institutional memory, such hard-won self-knowledge as you'd been able to eke at 14 or 16 or 18 or whenever you threw in your lot with a booker who liked what you'd always hated about your nose

– while curly-haired Scientologist teen sitcom actors who carried wads of hundreds secured with rubber bands lectured you in night clubs about the additive contents of Red Bull

– & you wandered this earth selling the rights to your image for a living

– while enjoying unimpeachable cultural security

– & occupying a position of abject & total disempowerment.

Helen of Sparta

[**W**]hereupon she went || home to Tennessee || paid back the || blue she'd stolen || sought the quiet life || owned cats || nervous little moggies || following her round || noses pyramidical || wind-sniffing || expecting each morn || to find the house || burned down around their ears || prows of Attic triremes || beached in the magnolia beds || birthing hoplite intrusion || & burnished shields || to bear home the corpses || all to do with trade war || somebody told her || in the nail salon || mercantile supremacy || cooked up over || a game of backgammon || in the shadow of || the Monastariki mosque || things life & death || that meant little || or nothing to || stalking paws pursuing || frightened mice or || a teenage girl || trying on her jewellery || at the mirror.

The Dance (Greta pt. ii)

[B]egins
in the street to   a soundtrack of
tribal percussion   & barking dogs

the dance begins
with lowered eyes &   click-bait articles in
your social media feed   'the 9 habits of women
who always stay beautiful'   you own your virtue
it is all that you have   & you are not afraid to
let it shine for all to see   to defend your modesty
with a sharp tongue   to make him crawl

the dance begins
in Thule, with time   to exercise, journal or
sing of faithful love   with a casket that
crawls out from   its cupboard, makes
you feel cared for   & valued, creeps into
your thoughts &   murmurs words as sweet
as ice-cream

the dance begins
in a garden where   your dreams are hung
in tatters from the   trees, where you exercise
to know your body   from a wild wood, where
the red thread that   joined you to the likelihood
of being in love was   broken, where a wolf peeps
through a crack in   the door & his eyes are
matchsticks

the dance begins
at the spinning-wheel
new hobby, the humility
& confidence once
wrap himself around
better to taste your skin
into your flesh, learning
lead you down corridors
speak in tongues, that

the dance begins
& we put on our
robes & wait for your
            knife.

with a personal goal or
to learn something new
mastered, to make him
you like a fresh towel, the
& read the fortune sewn
to own your mistakes will
with sharp hands, that
whisper that they care

glass smiles & bloody
appointment with the

Mater Dolorosa

[M]other of
sorrows, wounded
seven times, heart
pierced by seven
swords, these being

– *presumably* –

all they could
find room for.

The Soldier (Valentin)

[**O**]h my medals, my flags, insignia of
rank & shields – how I love to fuck

the one & be married to the others
in church on Sundays – make me great

again, for when I look in the mirror
I see a goat's horns butting the glass

I have followed my cock like a
compass needle through the maze of

my prejudice but it is just a thin, red
thread in my hand – I long to be

bull-horned & sire many golden
calves but all of my wealth is given

out in promissory notes in exchange
for my service in this army of children

our trumpets are louder than cannon
but we can be mighty when no-one is

watching – I have hidden beneath the
skirts of my family's reputation all

my life & I am afraid of the coming
light – my face only looks backwards

because all of my futures were written
in the past – I am a soldier because that

is what I was told I would be & I haven't
the courage to be any more of a man.

Altarpiece (This small world)

[**T**]his small world
huddled at the base of
its empty cross, where you crouch
shivering without him, this

small world
made of piety & steel wool
an empty
little cell with narrow windows which the
light must never enter, this small

world
of pumice stone &
regulation, thoughts scrubbed clean with
lye, its hawthorn tongue
demanding penance

     gather this unwanted child in your
               apron
   heedless of the small crying it makes, carry it
               to the fire
read the judgment of this world in its ashes

            in velvet
         collar & silver watch
             chain, I
       saw him at his prayers
              eyes
      discharging milky plasm
       brow mopped with a
      silk kerchief, a plateful

of roast lamb before him, this small
man beside his window
rocking steadily to & fro
listening out for
petticoats' swish & ladies' footfall
muttering, his flies unbuttoned.

The Cathedral (Greta pt. iii)

[S]tepping to the altar
so full of innocence

day of wrath, that day
will dissolve the world
into cinders

mood. forever

men with
glossy, black holes
where their eyes should be

whose blood is that on your
doorstep

thus when the judge holds court
whatever is hidden will appear

your reflection is not your own

your body in profile, eyes narrowed
raised from the quietness of ashes, into
the flames

his head in your hands

nothing will remain unavenged

      "I wish, I wish I had
      a bouquet of flowers for a head"

you didn't look
like yourself, the make-up was

too heavy, telling you to smile
in a fake way

breathing his air, a shrine to your
autonomy

you were flattered by
his desire

U told the truth. U lost the anchor
No hurt. No Upset. All energy bunny
now that it's sunny

      "I wish, I wish I had
      a bouquet of flowers for a head"

debating who owned these
images of you, the countless naked
pictures on his phone

You thought you were a mind
But you're a body

You thought you could have a public life
But your private life is here to sabotage you

You thought you had power
So let us destroy you.

The Cherries

– [A] red bowl
Mm hmm, oh yeah

– colour itself is
a degree of darkness

– would you like a
taste?

– at its heart, a cold
stone

– at its stone, a cold
cold heart

– in its flesh, a
withered little stalk

– but let's not think
too much on that *Mm
hmm, oh no*

– put it in your
mouth, let its succour
bruise your tongue
its flavour guide you
into cool shade under-
neath the orchard's
boughs

– bravery is such a
heavy weight in your
belly, such a length
of rope around your

conscience, pulling
you down beneath
the dark, dark water

Mm hmm, oh yeah

– but cowardice is
the sweetest vice
    of all, my love.

Mm hmm, oh yeah

The Stairs

[**O**]n & up
upon their backs you
climb, towards your
high ideal. Your foot
treads lightly with *oh*
such loving weight!
Aren't they the lucky
ones – Lili, Susanna
Gretchen, sisters all –
each with their own
parts to play in this
your great endeavour?
Is it not proof of your
impossible humanity
that stepping gently
on their love makes
your ascent so hard?

– well, *harder* at least
a little slower, maybe
a pause or two for
reflection on the way –

– but you'll get there
all the same, no doubt
over their dead bodies.

Walpurgis Night

[S]oul snatched out of body || a spiral into the abyss || separation of astral self & ego || *hey ho away we go* || pick up some broken glass || from the ground || & cut your arms || a threshold guardian || realm of magic || realm of dreams || escape the vulgarity of || the daylight quotidian || this utter night sensation factory || a cornucopia into || the infinite black above || a palace of becoming || a church for people || who have fallen from grace || confound your mind's || surveillance geography || nothing is fixed || hundreds of writhing bodies || each a lightning rod of intensity || each limit-human || swallowing all the energy || & insatiably wanting more || mountainous bass beats || each body-shaking sound || decaying into the next || all that is solid || melting into air || into the essential being || of the super-sensible || channeled into the essence || of the spiritual world || with its mix of magnitude || & fathomless dark || transcendental intensity || of space || & unforgiving techno || lose yourself in *erewhon* || the liberating nowhere || accessible within the here & now || the morphogenetic experience || of overflowing bounds || becoming animal || becoming other || the smoke & the sweat || & the heat & the blue || & pink strobe || everything looks different || bouquets of white lilies || under brutal concrete walls || faces flash up || & meld into each other || there are a lot of freaks || & that's a word || you apply to yourself as well || lord of the night || aglow in the mountains || among the naked tattooed flesh || lit dimly through the party || simultaneously inviting & || denying your gaze || hear the voice of one || who has clambered || for three hundred years || shouting *'fuck me!'* to || the rigidly capitalist version of truth || enforced in every city || a penis pierced to || the point of mutilation || exaggerated versions || of yourself emerging || through unforeseen encounters || birds migrating || across the Brocken || & buried in an ivy-fringed shallow grave || the origins of much || of the world are || brought to light || delicacy sensitivity & play || more potent than brute force || where history is ripped open || new histories become possible.

The Tavern (pt. ii)

[**W**]hereupon Goethe climbs
onto the table, waving his
glass like a herald's trumpet
calling for a toast

– 'to the vision of artists
the genius of science & the
sinews of industry!'. 'I die
content', he shouts, 'a happy
man to see such changes in
the world'.

– '& when you die'
says Marlowe, 'you will
probably be damned' –

– 'but even death', Tsvetaeva
says, 'won't be enough to keep
him quiet'.

The Sirens

[O]f course, we are not the
heroes of this tale, only women
distrusted women, seductive women
beguiling women, that we are

well now. let's grave the record right
put away your tombstone, hear our song

believe not   braggart Ulysses
believe not   coward Adam

it's not we nameless women who've entreated
men through ages to their deaths. Not us, defamed
by poets, who mansplain you to Elysium

of course, we are not the heroes of this
tale. Heroes need swords blood war &
death to make a world. We need only song

why would we many onevoiced sing except
to guide lovers husbands fathers safe to shore?
why would we cut our hair & weave our nets
if not to feed our little ones?

believe not   braggart Ulysses
believe not   coward Adam
believe   your mothers sisters daughters

grace us not with names but name us graces & not sirens
name us women. Take the beeswax from your ears & heed
our song

Things might go better, next time, if you do.

The Pharsalian Fields/by the Aegean Sea

[**P**]ower always meets
a greater power, time
becomes dense, Homunculus
in his diving bell, preparing to descend

a sea of 200,000 cypress trees, mixed
from legion materials, alive with generations
of political flyers, communist trade unionists
chanting, *'The people will speak'*

placards, a general strike, 'We are insolvent &
we must embrace our foreign ghosts', bringing
the country to a Papandreou standoff, the Aegean
like a gravestone, fires redden & glow

riot police keep guard over
contested terrain, armies of ideas
clash mercilessly, a fiscal waterboarding behind
closed doors, Erichtho pulls on her gas mask

'so many times already come again, so
many times & will into eternity', accused of
talking about economics

a warning to the government, to boss
the northern witches, Angela watching
from her stone, Wolfgang all serene, a thousand years
of computerised astrology, there's nothing new

none will who got by force & rules
by force allow it any man, bulletproof barriers refuse
emergency lines of credit, legislators break ranks
one eye & just one tooth between them

an academic with Marxist roots
wants what cannot be, in a T-shirt with an outline
of Texas on the front, a shining light flies
through the night, is thrown upon the rocks

all hell breaks loose, a mountain
rises up into Syntagma Square, the Eurogroup
comes near, explodes & rains down deficit, rains down
the junk of priests & monopolies

Nereus sweeps up broken glass, all
that his spirit has seen, the air chokes for breath
what difference did advising ever make?
fixed between communiques & steel shutters, caught
in a death embrace, broken into pieces against
the bright throne.

The Bell

[T]ake out your eyes,
this is for your own
good & ours

We are agreed, you
& all of us, all of
us & you, that this
is the right thing to
do

Imagine a clock, its
hands turning, hours
passing – though you
can no longer see

– all is well – its hands
still turn, the hours
still pass

– & now that you are
blind, we have added
more hours to the day

– now that you no longer
need the light, all the hours
of the night will be the day
& all the hours of the day
will be the day as well

This is the bargain that
we made, the cracked
bell that we have struck –

these are our last words
on the matter & if they
are not, then those words
will be the last

– what matters is that
we stand together, all
of us & you, you &
all of us, & go as
one

– into the darkness.

Philomen & Baucis

[**W**]hose fate was
ordained by one
who, maybe, on
hearing the fable
of the widow's mite
took from it this
lesson, that it is a
good & noble
thing for those
with least to give
up all they have.

The Factory

[A] line, a line as long as infinity can be
stretched & being stretched, can be

pulled, a rope through block & tackle
to lift innumerable weights, a queue of

wretched bodies waiting to put their
shoulders to the wheel, to walk the

endless uphill treadmill only to find
themselves upon some false summit

become a weight to brake a load rolling
downhill, become a hammer swung to

beat others of their ilk into new shapes
become the metal laid beneath the

hammer to be beaten out of being one
thing into another, to be loaded into

crates or boxes, carried upon trucks to
another station on the factory floor

whereupon they are unpacked, set
upright, called into the line & put

to the work of making or remaking, of
lifting or of being broken, all the while

being told they should be grateful that
this, at least, is existence with a purpose.

The Road

[T]his road
you're standing on
from over that hill
from wherever it's
been from wherever
            you set out

 – *this* road you're standing on

we built this road

shovelled aggregate
for the base course
bitumen man laid the
best pavements since
the Pleistocene era
heat stressed 'til you
could fry an
            egg on it

– *millions of millions* of wheel passes

falling out of Eden
get the hot tar
bubbling, shovelfuls
of mountainside
chewing up God's
creation like beans
on a fork, ready for
            the roller

stretch over that hill-top
down the other side
day after further still
you get the picture

– man loves to build roads
where they go doesn't
            matter.

Tom Walker

[**A**] time of paper credit
speculators light cigars with government bills
cut about with pocket knives, to test the depth of fat
dreams of Mar-a-Largo in their eyes.

Old Tom Walker went out to the woods
names of rich colonialists carved into the trees
dropped a couple of holes to keep things friendly
won himself a share in Bill Kidd, the Pirate's treasure
all for the right price, of course

a house, a car & a new career in television
a dead woman's heart & lungs wrapped up in an apron
an unkindness of knives that twisted in his mouth
Brioni suits, cut wide across the shoulder
finasteride & cold-cream on a polished truncheon
getting the help to cinch him into a leather sling

lived in mortal terror of the collection plate
his best horse buried in its saddle, upside down
one bible in his pocket, another on his desk
when the TV cameras came by looking for a story, he cried
'the devil take me, if I have made a cent'

you fell on him like a brigade of lightning
stuffed a thousand Georgia ballots in his mouth
dragged him off behind a Pontiac Firebird
left a ragged smear of laughter on the wind.

The Author

[U]nlovely
cabinet of man, skin draped
& tightly pinned across his cavities
shelves & compartments, where he keeps his files
names of those who have done him wrong
things he wants not to forget

a heap of parts
tottering on tripedal legs, tiny feet
always saying 'no' to something
scraping other peoples' ideas off their pages
with a blunt thumb
        of knife –

that are written on our flesh – hold us close
enough to the fire that our hair begins to singe

& see them appear on our skin, in letters that
are also scars – words that he takes away in

canisters to be weighed, that are all that's
left of our articles of faith, that were kept in

our library of possible futures, indexed under
'still to come', that we will carve into all of

the monuments we raise to those who don't
        live to see their moment realised –

– that are bought & paid for in arrears
always in arrears, always behind & creeping up on him
beseeching things, wailing & wailing across the floor
'Father, why have you
        abandoned us?'

The Gates

What was it like for you
to wake from the dream, to be
no longer seized by that outbreak of mass hysteria
to find the past unwritten
palimpsest peeled back
dull bones of phenomenal reality exposed
chimneys smoking

to no longer run on wolves' paws
lap from clear streams that chuckle through city streets
sleep beneath trees whose roots crack concrete pavements
whose branches & canopies burst through roofs
beneath a sun that is every colour & none
beneath a sky that spins with the giddy intensity
of children playing

to no longer feel the grass bend with the weight of morning dew
the earth's warmth as it comforts seams of buried coal
the shyness of oil, undisturbed & sleeping peacefully
beneath a sea-bed alive with the calligraphy of coral
the traffic of passing fish

to no longer be one, in our perception of each other
to re-assert that boundary, feel the door slam shut
no longer have room, within our skins, within our heads
for anyone but ourselves, the expulsion of all that
an act of spitting out, undoing
falling on our knees again
naked & ashamed, outside the gates
of what might have been Eden.

The Thorn Bushes

[N]eedn't be good soil, deep
loam or anything like that.
A scruffing of dirt, an after-
thought on the rock, the
barest covering is fine. We
are resourceful beasts, bred
to thrive where least expected
on ground where other softer
needier plants would suffer.
Suffering is our birth-right
beat us with the sun, leave us
to thirst, give us no more rain
than you would use to wet
your lips & we'll be fine.
Ignore us, pay no notice to
the fact that there are more
of us now than when you
last visited or – if & only
if, it suits you – winnow us
with fire. Serve notice of
your intent to repossess this
half-acre of hillside rock
for a short time, end our
tenancy, give our children
to the wind that they may
sow themselves like dragons'
teeth across the world. No
matter, we'll be back again.
Fittest of all growing things
to crown the head of Christ
your saviour & just like
him, it's said, after a few
days, we will rise.

Author's Note

I thought it might be helpful to offer some explanation as to what all this is supposed to have been about.

'Mephistopheles' is a collection of poems, most (but not all) of which are loosely based on the Faust myth as told by Christopher Marlowe in the sixteenth century & Johann Wolfgang von Goethe in the eighteenth & nineteenth. In part, it is also an argument with the 'Great Man' theory of history & Max Weber's concept of charismatic authority. Both of which feel as though they have been put into stark relief by recent political & other developments, in the USA & elsewhere in the world.

Weber defined 'charisma' as "A certain quality of an individual personality, by virtue of which he is set apart from ordinary men and treated as endowed with supernatural, superhuman, or at least specifically exceptional powers or qualities." This, broadly speaking, can be said to describe Faust, in both Marlowe's & Goethe's treatments.

My 'argument' is that this kind of authority is not innate but is appropriated at a cost, one usually born by others. Examples abound throughout the Faust story, but two of them might be Mephistopheles themself, in Marlowe's version & Goethe's doomed love interest, Greta.

Whatever else they may be, it is clear from Marlowe's text that Mephistopheles is not an authority figure. They are a go-between, bringing messages from senior decision-makers in Hell to Faustus & back again. When Faustus speaks of repenting his bargain with the Devil, Mephistopheles becomes agitated & it's reasonable to assume that the penalty imposed upon them for letting Faustus get away would be severe.

If we extend this surmise further – by borrowing from Books One & Two of John Milton's *Paradise Lost*, where Satan's army cast down from Heaven arrive in Hell – we arrive at the idea of Mephistopheles as a foot-soldier in a defeated army (perhaps with little alternative to service) driven out of their home by the equivalent of a technologically superior force. They may have power, but they have only limited agency.

In amongst some general scene-setting, many of the poems in the first third of this collection (from 'The War in Heaven' to 'Farewell') are either based on, or are commentaries on, this idea: Mephistopheles as precarious employee. The point being, that Faustus' 'charismatic authority' derives not so much from his innate quality, as it does from the [likely enforced] labour of one with little choice in whom they serve & how.

The rest of the book (from 'The Algorithm' to the end) applies a similar logic to Goethe's broader canvas. A sequence of ten poems ('Greta' to 'The Stairs') draws this out with especial reference to the character of Greta. Greta's insertion by Goethe into the Faust-story being an especially brutal example of the trope of 'fridging'[1] – violently killing-off a female character in order to inspire the protagonist to subsequent 'great' deeds. As before, some poems act as commentary, while others stay closer to the over-arching narrative.

A final sequence of poems ('The Road' to 'The Thorn Bushes') seeks to bring some of these ideas into the modern era & places them against the backdrop of late-stage capitalism.[2]

---

1   See: Women in Refrigerators (website): http://www.lby3.com/wir

2   For example, 'The Pharsalian Fields/by the Aegean Sea' replays events from the Greek sovereign debt crisis against the backdrop of Goethe's set-piece Classical Walpurgis Night.

Like 'Jan Twardowski' earlier in the book, 'Jack Walker' borrows a popular folk retelling of a Faust story (in Jack's case, by Washington Irving) in order to make cheap (but cathartic!) mockery of a certain, recent United States President.

In these closing poems, & across the collection overall, I was indebted to Marshall Berman's conception of Faust as the epitome of modernity – the great 'developer'[3]. In this context, development has the tenor inherent in the idea of a 'developed' & 'developing world', & the implicit/explicit imbalance in power relations between the two. Michael Swanwick's 'Jack Faust' was useful here also.

The last poem in the book 'The Thorn Bushes' sounds a final, hopeful chord. In producing this collection, I took (as I often do, when times are dark) comfort from the activism & comradeship of others – some living, some now sadly passed. Modesty (theirs, not mine) precludes me from naming names but, if there is any truth in that apocryphal quote attributed to Margaret Mead about 'thoughtful, committed citizens', I expect them to be members of that small (but mighty!) group.

---

3   See: Berman, Marshall; 'All That is Solid Melts into Air' (pub. Verso, 2010)

Notes

General

◊   References to *Faust (Pt I)* by Johan Wolfgang Von Goethe are to the Penguin Classics edition, 2005.

◊   References to *Faust (Pt II)* by Johan Wolfgang Von Goethe are to the Penguin Classics edition, 2009.

◊   References to *Doctor Faustus* by Christopher Marlowe are to the Methuen edition, 1965 (reprinted by Routledge, 1988).

The War in Heaven (after Milton)

◊   This poem was collaged from the following source material:

◊   *Paradise Lost* by John Milton, Book VI (Penguin Classics, 2000).
◊   The Wikipedia entry for the video game series *God of War*.
◊   "The Gulf War myth: A study of the press coverage of the 1991 Gulf conflict" [PhD Thesis; City University, London], by Richard Keeble (Pub. online at: https://core.ac.uk/reader/42628214).
◊   An interview with the writer James Kelman (Pub. online by 3AM Magazine at: https://www.3ammagazine.com/3am/the-war-against-silence-an-interview-with-james-kelman/).
◊   "A Cold Coming" by Tony Harrison (Pub. online by The Guardian newspaper at: https://www.theguardian.com/theguardian/2003/feb/14/features11.g2).

The Agency

◊   'Big Other' refers to the concept used by psychoanalyst & psychiatrist Jacques Lacan to designate radical alterity, an 'otherness' which transcends the illusory otherness of the imaginary because it cannot be assimilated through identification. Lacan equated this radical alterity with language & the law.

Prologue in Heaven

◊   In the brief given to artist Graham Sutherland for his large tapestry 'Christ in Glory in the Tetramorph', which hangs in the nave of the New Cathedral, Coventry, Cathedral Provost Richard Howard told the artist, *"[D]epicting the face of Christ would be difficult, it may come to you to conceive an English face, universal at the same time"*.

The Bells

◊   Responds to & quotes from *Faust (Pt. I)*; 762 – 784.
◊   *'Memnosyne'* refers to the Greek Goddess of memory & mother of the 9 muses (one of which was Euterpe, muse of music & lyric poetry).

The Red Pill

◊   Responds to *Doctor Faustus;* Scene 1, lines 1-165.

The Interview

◊   Borrows lines from the popular hymn, 'The Lord of the Dance', written by Sydney Carter (1963).

Mephistopheles

◊   Previously published with a different title
[*Mephistopheles (before their 1ˢᵗ date with Faustus*] in Issue 29 of
Riggwelter Magazine. Thanks to the editor for their support.

The Fall

◊   '*Wittenberg*' refers to the University in Germany, where
Marlowe locates Faustus at the opening of his play.

Farewell

◊   Modifies & responds to Mephistopheles' line from
Doctor Faustus; Scene 19, line 98), "Fools that will laugh on earth,
must weep in hell", while taking inspiration (& the villanelle
form) from Dylan Thomas' '*Do not go gentle into that good night*'.

The Algorithm

◊   This poem & **The Wager** which follows respond (in
part) to *Faust (Pt. I); 1692 – 1766* – the scene in which Faust agrees
his strange wager with Mephistopheles telling him "If ever I
settle on a bed of ease / Let me be done for there and then".

The Dolls

◊   Includes references to divers scenes from *Doctor Faustus*
– encounters with the Pope (Scene 8), the German Emperor
(Scene 12) & the moment when Faustus conjures horns onto the
head of court attendant Benvolio (Scene 12, lines 70-118).

The Tavern

◊   '*Tsvetaeva*' refers to the Russian poet Marina Tsvetaeva,
whose appearance in this collection was inspired by her poem
'*Bound for Hell*'.

Jan Twardowski

◊   Refers to the character from Polish folklore & another version of the Faust myth – wherein Jan (or 'Pan') Twardowski enters a pact with the devil in exchange for magical powers.
◊   *'Painted with honey & gold leaf'* here & elsewhere in the poem some of Twardowski's antics are borrowed from the performance practice of artist Joseph Beuys.

The Seven Sins

◊   Responds to *'Doctor Faustus'*, Scene 6, lines 114-169, where Lucifer & Beelzebub arrive from Hell to turn Faustus from thoughts of repentance & beguile him with sights to 'delight his soul'.

The Witch's Kitchen

◊   Responds to *Faust (Pt I)*; lines 2337 – 2604 (set in the titular kitchen), to make a sort of prologue to the Helen/Greta sequence that follows.
◊   *'Pinochle'* refers to the card game.

Greta (after Mayakovsky)

◊   Inspired by the account of Russian poet Vladimir Mayakovsky's love affair with Lilya ('Lili') Brik as told in Bengt Jangfeldt's *'Mayakovsky – A Biography'* (University of Chicago Press, 2015).
◊   *'Zhukovsky street'* is a street in St Petersburg, Russia.

Helen

◊ Collaged from the article *'I Am The Anonymous Model'* by Jenna Sauers (Pub. online at: https://jezebel.com/i-am-the-anonymous-model-5317761) together with references to 'Doctor Faustus', Sc.18, lines. 99-118 – where Helen's image is conjured by Mephistopheles to dissuade Faustus from repentance.

◊ *'Menelaus'* refers to the King of Sparta in Greek mythology, brother of Agamemnon & the 'cuck' whose wife Helen is stolen away by the Trojan Prince Paris, leading to the Trojan War.

◊ *'Lech Walesa'* refers to the statesman, Nobel Prize-winner & first Polish President to be elected by popular vote.

Helen of Sparta

◊ Plays a little with the fact that, while Helen was Queen to Menelaus of Sparta, Sparta is also a city in, & the county seat of White County, Tennessee.

◊ *'Monastariki Mosque'*, refers to the Tzisdarakis Mosque in Monastariki Square, Athens, Greece which now houses the Museum of Modern Greek Culture.

The Dance (Greta, pt. ii)

◊ *'Click-bait articles'* refers to *'9 habits of women who are always attractive'* (Pub. online at: https://www.mychicobsession.com/habits-of-women-who-are-always-attractive/) & its ilk.

◊ *'Thule'* refers to the most northerly location named in classical literature, which acquired the metaphorical meaning of 'a distant place beyond the borders of the known world'.

Mater Dolorosa

◊ Responds to *Faust (Pt I)*; lines 3587 – 3619, taking inspiration from the iconographic image of Mary, mother of Christ pierced by seven swords referenced in this scene.

The Soldier (Valentin)

◊ Responds to *Faust (Pt I)*; lines 3620 – 3775, in which Greta's brother Valentin brawls with Faust & dies, cursing his sister.

◊ This poem was previously published online by The Babel Tower Notice Board at: https://www.thebabeltowernoticeboard.com/featured-writing/ three-poems-by-chris-boyland. With thanks to the editors for their support.

The Cathedral (Greta Pt. iii)

◊ This poem was collaged from the following source material:

◊ Faust (Pt I), lines 3776-3834.
◊ *'Buying Myself Back: When does a model own her own image'* by Emily Ratajkowski (Pub. online by The Cut at: https://www. thecut.com/article/emily-ratajkowski-owning-my-image-essay. html).
◊ Facebook post by Rebecca Solnit (Pub. on the author's Facebook page at https://www.facebook.com/rebecca.solnit/ posts/10157374665780552).

The Stairs

◊ *'Lili'* refers to Anna Elisabeth "Lili" Schönemann, described as Goethe's "first great love" & to whom he was betrothed before breaking off the engagement.
◊ *'Susanna'* refers to Susanna Margaretha Brandt, beheaded in 1772 for murdering her infant child. Goethe was working as a lawyer in the same town (Frankfurt) at the time & Susanna's death is widely taken as the inspiration for the character of Greta.

Walpurgis Night

◊ Responds to *Faust (Pt I)*; lines 3835 – 4040, collaged together with text found in articles on the Berlin nightclub & 'Techno Cathedral', Berghain.

◊ This poem was previously published online by The Babel Tower Notice Board. at: https://www.thebabeltowernoticeboard.com/featured-writing/three-poems-by-chris-boyland With thanks to the editors for their support.

The Sirens

◊ Creatures of Greek myth & epic poetry (see *The Odyssey*; Book 12, lines 39 – 54 & 154 – 200), who appear in the 'Classical Walpurgis Night' sequence in *Faust (Pt II)*.

◊ This poem was previously published in the pamphlet, *User Stories* (Stewed Rhubarb Press, 2020).

The Pharsalian Fields/by the Aegean Sea

◊ This poem was collaged from the following source material:

◊ *Faust (Pt II; Act 2, 'Classical Walpurgis Night'),* with quotations from lines 7005-7024 & 7676-7695.

◊ *The Greek Warrior: How a radical finance minister took on Europe – and failed* (Pub. online by The New Yorker at: https://www.newyorker.com/magazine/2015/08/03/the-greek-warrior, 2015).

◊ *'Papandreou'* refers to George Andreas Papandreou, former Prime Minister of Greece (2009-2011).

◊ *'Erichtho'* refers to the Thessalian witch from classical literature.

◊ *'Angela'* refers to Angela Merkel, former Chancellor of Germany (2005-2021).

◊ *'Wolfgang'* refers to Wolfgang Schäuble, former Finance Minister of Germany (2009-2017).

◊   *'Syntagma Square'*, the central, civic square in Athens, Greece.

◊   *'the Eurogroup'* refers to the committee of finance ministers of countries using the Euro.

◊   *'Nereus'* refers to the sea-god from classical Greek myth, who had the gift of prophesy.

Philomen & Baucis

◊   Responds to the account in *Faust (Pt II; Act 5)*, of this amiable old couple's murder at the hands of Mephistopheles.

Tom Walker

◊   Inspired by *'The Devil and Tom Walker'* from *Tales of a Traveller* by Washington Irving (1824), like 'Jan Twardowski', an alternative folk-version of the Faust myth & also by more recent personalities & events in American politics.

CD Boyland is a poet, visual poet, and editor who lives in Cumbernauld, near Glasgow. His pamphlets are *User Stories* (2020); *Vessel* (2022); *SMC_* (also 2022) and *Ptchdk_* (2023). Other work has been published in magazines and anthologies such as: 3AM Magazine, Beir Bua, Gutter, The Interpreter's House, The North and New Writing Scotland. He is a Trustee of the Edwin Morgan Trust and also co-edits The Glasgow Review of Books.